THE
APRIL
BABY

THE
April
BABY

★

Noel Streatfeild

First published in 1959
This edition published in 2023 by Headline Home
an imprint of Headline Publishing Group

1

Cataloguing in Publication Data is available from the British Library

Hardback ISBN 978 1 0354 0845 0
eISBN 978 1 0354 0846 7

Typeset in 14.75/15pt Centaur MT Pro by Jouve (UK), Milton Keynes

Printed and bound in Great Britain by Clays Ltd, Elcograf S.p.A.

HEADLINE PUBLISHING GROUP
An Hachette UK Company
Carmelite House
50 Victoria Embankment
London EC4Y 0DZ

www.headline.co.uk
www.hachette.co.uk

CONTENTS

The April Baby   1

Names for the April Baby   7

Gifts for the April Baby   15

Under what Stars was my Baby born?   19

Babies born on the same Day as your Baby   27

The Upbringing of April Babies of
          the Past   35

Two Royal April Babies   47

Distinguished April Babies   53

Games for the April Baby   65

An April Child in Fiction   68

Letters from April Children   71

Rhymes for the April Baby   76

Goodnight to the April Baby   82

YOUR baby has arrived. Telephone bells have been ringing, messages have passed from mouth to mouth, and all the questions have been asked and some of them answered. How is she? Did she have a bad time? Is it a boy or a girl? What colour are the eyes? Is there any hair? What did it weigh when it was born?

And now the day has come when you are to be allowed visitors, and at once the problem arises, what present shall be brought to you?

April has never been an easy month for flowers, perhaps because Easter, usually in April, sucks in so many for church decorations. There are of course primroses, jonquils, and polyanthus, but likely enough mother and baby have received so many of these, that long ago all the suitably sized vases and pots have been used up. Tulips are on the market, but they are still expensive, and there is something most disheartening about spending rather more than you can afford, only to find that the room or ward already looks like an exhibition stand at the Chelsea Flower Show.

If most of us gave way to our inclinations we would, on hearing the baby has arrived, rush off to the nearest toy shop, and buy the silkiest, fluffiest toy we can see. Each year at Christmas time, men and women in search of space-ships, guns, and brain-searching games, can be seen casting longing glances at the soft toy department, unable to find an excuse to

look because there isn't a baby. Now that reason no longer exists, what fun to choose something enchanting. But does mother really want that real fur white rabbit with pink velvet ears? For baby doesn't, and won't for a long while yet. It is hard to resist that lion cub, it will look so sweet lying on the pramcover. But will it lie on the pramcover, or will it be put away until baby is old enough to enjoy it? No, soft toys are out.

There is no present nicer than something to wear. It is spring, soon it will be summer, the trees are bursting out in leaves and blossoms, and we in new clothes – or are we? For those who can afford it the diaphanous nightgowns with matching negligees are charming presents, but how many can afford them? How many know that for themselves there will be no new clothes, and that the

coming of spring means bundling up last year's clothes for the little woman round the corner to alter?

It is years of facing this problem, 'What present shall I take?' that has resulted in this book. What does every mother of a new baby talk and think about? Baby, of course. So here between two covers is collected information about April babies, to amuse her.

Few parents need help in choosing names; usually the difficulty is to decide which to choose from the abundance offered. Shall the grandparents be flattered, and if so, which? What about the godparents? Having selected a rich one, wouldn't it be a good idea to draw further attention to the godchild by giving it the same name? Then of course there are family names. But there are always a few parents who have still not made up their minds when they are standing beside the font. It is all very well calling the baby Mary Jane or Marmaduke before it arrives, but do they really want the child labelled Mary Jane or Marmaduke for life? For such parents there is a selection of names to choose from, all having something to do with April.

As an offering to all mothers of April babies, here laid out for their perusal are the characteristics their baby is supposed to have because it was born under the sign of Aries or comes under the influence of Taurus. How odd, the mother may think, that so many artists, both interpretive and creative, should have been Taurus babies, which is supposed to mean that they do not dream, but live fully in the external world. And did that writer of the gentle and fantastic, Sir James Barrie, really have an aggressive spirit as, born under the sign of Aries, he should have had? Certainly the zodiac signs are something on which a mother might well meditate, thinking of course, not of those others born on the same day, but of the important newcomer now added to the list.

NAMES
for the
APRIL
BABY

APRIL or *Avril* is a popular name for an April baby, but some may feel it rather an obvious choice, so here are suggestions for April as the spring month signifying renewal and birth. There are several names which mean renewal. *René* and *Renée* mean 'born again'. *Eugene* and *Owen* mean 'well-born'. *Eustace* 'fruitful' and *Ephraim* 'doubly fruitful'. *Florian* and *Flory* mean 'blooming', *Reuben* 'renewer' and *Vernon* 'flourishing'. *Virgil*

means 'spring-like', and *Vivian* 'alive'. Here are some girls' names: *Eugenia* means 'well-born', *Natalia* and *Natalie* both mean 'birth'.

Thinking of birth reminds us of the men who have devoted their lives to working for the health of babies. William Harvey for one – *Harvey* means 'warrior-war' – and John Hunter, a famous surgeon of the 18th century: *Hunter* means what it says, and could be a good name for a boy.

Taurus is the April sign of the zodiac. *Bevis* is a name connected with it, meaning 'bull'.

The Romans consecrated the 1st of April to Venus, goddess of love; there are a number of names connected with love. *Amy* and *Morna* both mean 'beloved'. *Amabel, Annabel, Annabella* and *Mabel* all mean 'lovable'. *Amanda* is a popular name at present, it means 'fit to be loved'. *Lida* means 'the people's love'. *Charis, Charissa, Charity, Elma, Minna,* and *Minnie* mean 'love', and so, though it makes you think of spring blossom, does *Cherry*. Close to this in meaning is *Desiree* which means 'desired'.

The month of April is rich in saints' days. The apostle which legend gives for the month is Philip. *Philip* means 'horse-lover'. Names with similar meanings are *Caspar* or *Casper* 'horseman', and *Hippolytus* which means 'letting horses loose', but it is unlikely any modern mother would want to christen her child Hippolytus.

The 3rd of April is St Richard's Day. *Richard* means 'stern ruler'. The 4th of April is assigned to St Ambrose. *Ambrose* means 'immortal', and so do *Brush* and *Emrys*.

The 23rd is the day on which Shakespeare was born. Here are some names taken from his plays. *Beatrice* means 'bringer of joy', *Bianca* 'white', *Celia* 'the heavens', *Cordelia* 'daughter of the sea', *Diana* 'moon goddess', *Hermione* 'daughter of Hermes', *Juliet* 'downy', *Miranda* 'worthy of admiration', *Olivia* 'olive', *Ophelia* 'assistance', *Portia* 'a sow' (fancy that!); *Rosalind* means 'fair as a rose'. For boys *Anthony* means 'inestimable', *Benedick* 'blessed', *Bertram* 'bright raven', *Duncan*

'brown warrior', *Edmund* 'rich protection', *Ferdinand* 'venturous journey', *Henry* 'home ruler', *Horatio* 'punctual', *Humphrey* 'giant peace', *Lewis* 'famous war', *Lucius* 'the light', *Oliver* 'olive-tree', *Orlando* 'fame of the land', and *Sebastian* 'venerable'.

The 23rd is also probably the best known saint's day in the English calendar, for it is St George's Day. *George* means 'tiller of the soil'. The emblem of England worn on St George's Day is a red rose, so *Rose* is a charming choice for a girl.

The 25th of April is St Mark's Day. *Mark* means 'of Mars'.

Usually Easter is in April, and in the past it has been used as a name for both boys and girls. There are several names in use today which have meanings connected with this festival. *Stacy* and *Stacey* both mean 'resurrection', *Anastasia* 'having the elements of the Resurrection within', *Christian* 'a follower of Christ', or for girls *Christiana, Christina,* or *Christine* which have the same meaning.

Christopher means 'Christ-bearing', *Dominic or Dominica* 'of the Lord'. Lilies are always on the altar at Easter-time; *Sukey, Susan, Susanna, Susannah* and *Suzanne* all mean 'graceful white lily'.

April is the month when all the wild flowers are coming into bud. They say when you can cover seven daisies with one foot, summer has arrived. April is a little early for being able to do that, but a daisy is April's flower. It means 'day's eye'.

For mothers looking for an original April name how about *Cuckoo*? 'In April come he will.'

GIFTS
for the
APRIL
BABY

IF a godparent or any well-wisher wishes to give a piece of jewellery to the April baby, they should be rich, for the right stone is the diamond. Mothers of April babies should be proud to think their offspring have chosen so opulent a month, but there is a surprise connected with diamonds. Being such a well-known sign of wealth who could guess that the diamond is the emblem of innocence. My! My! That would surprise some people we know. Here is what Leonardus wrote about diamonds.

'The Virtue . . . is to repel Poison, tho' ever so deadly; is a Defence against the Arts of Sorcery; disperses vain Fears; enables to quell all Quarrels and Contentions; is a Help to Lunaticks, and such as are possess'd with the Devil; being bound to the left arm, it gives Victory over Enemies; it tames wild Beasts; it helps those who are troubled with Phantasms, and the Night-mare; and makes him that wears it bold and daring in his Transactions.'

The pretty old custom of knowing how to arrange wild flowers in a vase or bunch so that it brings a message is neglected nowadays. If, however, your baby should receive a bunch of moss, bearded crepis, primroses, daisies, and wood sorrel, here is what the present means:

Moss (maternal love), crepis (protect), primroses (early youth), daisies (innocence), wood sorrel (joy).

If your baby was born between the 1st and 20th of April read pages 22 and 23, but if between the 21st and the 30th April, skip to pages 24 and 25.

UNDER
WHAT STARS WAS
MY BABY
BORN?

ARIES
The Ram
21st March–20th April

TAURUS
The Bull
21st April–21st May

GEMINI
The Twins
22nd May–21st June

CANCER
The Crab
22nd June–23rd July

LEO
The Lion
24th July–23rd August

VIRGO
The Virgin
24th August–23rd September

LIBRA
The Scales
24th September–23rd October

SCORPIO
The Scorpion
24th October–22nd November

SAGITTARIUS
The Archer
23rd November–21st December

CAPRICORN
The Sea Goat
22nd December–20th January

AQUARIUS
The Water Bearer
21st January–19th February

PISCES
The Fishes
20th February–20th March

Aries — the Ram
21st March–20th April

ARIES, the most positive sign of the zodiac, gives a very progressive and aggressive spirit. Aries people are full of energy, hot and impulsive in their passions, large in their perceptions. Themselves basically ungovernable, they are ambitious to lead others and are more often than not well capable of doing so. They are generous, but not to the sacrifice of their own ends. People born under Aries may tend to be changeable and irritable, but where courage is needed they are, above all others, dauntless.

For the Aries Baby

Lucky to wear a ruby.
Lucky stone is flint.
Lucky metal is iron.
The Aries baby's colour is red.
Lucky number is 9.
Luckiest day of the week is Tuesday.

Taurus — the Bull
21st April–21st May

PEOPLE born under Taurus are notable for the quality of endurance. They are patient and tenacious workers, and have exceptionally good memories. No dreamers, they live fully in the external world. In personal relationships they tend to be domineering, and very jealous. Taureans are placid in temperament, slow to anger, but furious when provoked. They incline to ease and luxury, but as an objective for rather than a hindrance to their laboriousness.

For the Taurus Baby

Lucky to wear an emerald.
Lucky stones are malachite, turquoise,
   jade, alabaster.
Lucky metal is copper.
The Taurus baby's colour is green.
Lucky number is 6.
Luckiest day of the week is Friday.

BABIES BORN
ON
THE SAME DAY
AS
YOUR BABY

IS there any advantage to be gained from being born on a particular day? Is there any truth in what the astrologers say – that babies born under Aries are like this, and those under Taurus like that? Here is a list of people from all countries and walks of life who were born during April. Look through it before you make up your mind.

1st   William Harvey, 1578. Bismark, 1815. Edmond Rostand, 1864. Rachmaninoff, 1873. Edgar Wallace, 1875. Cicely Courtneidge, 1892.

2nd   Charlemagne, 742. Casanova, 1725. Hans Christian Andersen, 1805. Emile Zola, 1840. Alec Guinness, 1914.

3rd   Philip the Bold, 1245. George Herbert, 1593. Washington Irving, 1783. Leslie Howard, 1893. Marlon Brando, 1924.

4th   Maurice de Vlaminck, 1876. Pierre
       Fresnay, 1897. Duke of Beaufort, 1900.
       Captain Oliver Dawnay, 1920.

5th   Thomas Hobbes, 1588. Catherine I of
       Russia, 1689. Fragonard, 1732. Lord
       Lister, 1827. Swinburne, 1837. Spencer
       Tracy, 1900. Bette Davis, 1908. Gregory
       Peck, 1916.

6th   Alexander the Great, 356 B.C. James
       Mill, 1773. Harry Houdini, 1874.

7th   Saint Francis Xavier, 1506. William
       Wordsworth, 1770. Fourier, 1772. Sir
       Francis Chantrey, 1781. David Low,
       1891.

8th   Philip IV of Spain, 1605. Sir Adrian
       Boult, 1889. Dorothy Tutin, 1930.

9th   Duke of Monmouth, 1649. Baudelaire,
       1821. Sir James Barrie, 1860. Lenin, 1870.
       Paul Robeson, 1898. Hugh Gaitskell,
       1906. Robert Helpmann, 1909.

10th   James V of Scotland, 1512. Hugo
       Grotius, 1583. William Hazlitt, 1778.
       General Booth, 1829. Claire Boothe
       Luce, 1903.

11th   Margaret of Navarre, 1492. Christopher
       Smart, 1722. George Canning, 1770. Sir

Charles Hallé, 1819. John Northcote Nash, 1893.

12th   Anne of Denmark, 1577. Clare Leighton, 1899. Admiral Sir Rhoderick McGrigor, 1893.

13th   Isabella of Valois, 1545. Thomas Wentworth, Earl of Strafford, 1593. Lord North, 1732. Thomas Jefferson, 1743. Philip Louis, Duke of Orleans, 1747. Sir Robert Watson-Watt, 1892.

14th   Philip III of Spain, 1578. Christian Huygens, 1629. Earl of Athlone, 1874. Arnold Toynbee, 1889. B. R. Ambedkar, 1893. Sir John Gielgud, 1904.

15th   Leonardo Da Vinci, 1452. Sir James Clark Ross, 1800. Henry James, 1843. Viscount Bruce of Melbourne, 1883. Lady Violet Bonham-Carter, 1887.

16th   William the Silent of Orange, 1533. Sir John Franklin, 1786. Ford Maddox Brown, 1821. Anatole France, 1844. Earl of Halifax, 1881. Charles Chaplin, 1889. Lieut.-General Sir John Bagot Glubb, 1897. Peter Ustinov, 1921. Kingsley Amis, 1922.

17th   John Ford, 1586. Henry Vaughan, 1622.
John Pierpont Morgan, 1837. Maggie
Teyte, 1889. Thornton Wilder,
1897. William Holden, 1918. Lindsay
Anderson, 1923.

18th   Sir Arnold Lunn, 1888. Queen Frederika
of Greece, 1917.

19th   Edward Pellew, Viscount Exmouth,
1757. David Ricardo, 1772. Gustav
Fechner, 1801.

20th   Marcus Aurelius, 121 A.D. Sir John
Eliot, 1592. Napoleon III, 1808. Adolph
Hitler, 1889. Sir Donald Wolfit, 1902.

21st   Prince George of Denmark, 1653.
Charlotte Brontë, 1816. Henri de
Montherlant, 1896. Her Majesty The
Queen, 1926.

22nd   Isabella the Catholic, 1451. John
Carteret, Earl Granville, 1690. Henry
Fielding, 1707. Immanuel Kant, 1724.
Madame de Staël, 1766. Yehudi
Menuhin, 1916.

23rd   Louis IX of France, 1215. Shakespeare,
1564. Turner, 1775. Dame Ethel
Smyth, 1858. Max Planck, 1858.
Viscount Allenby, 1861. Prokofiev, 1891.

Margaret Kennedy, 1896. Ngaio Marsh, 1899.

24th   Edmund Cartwright, 1743. Anthony Trollope, 1815. Air Chief Marshal Lord Dowding, 1882. Sir Stafford Cripps, 1889. Elizabeth Goudge, 1900.

25th   Edward II, 1284. Oliver Cromwell, 1599. Walter de la Mare, 1873. Guglielmo Marconi, 1874. Ivor Brown, 1891. The Princess Royal, 1897. Sir Gladwyn Jebb, 1900.

26th   Maria de' Medici, 1573. David Hume, 1711. Emma Lady Hamilton, 1763. Alfred Krupp, 1812. Syngman Rhee, 1875. Sir Alliott Verdon-Roe, 1877.

27th   Mary Wollstonecraft Godwin, 1759. Maria Christina of Spain, 1806. Edward Gibbon, 1737. Samuel F. B. Morse, 1791. Herbert Spencer, 1820. Maurice Baring, 1874. Cecil Day-Lewis, 1904.

28th   Edward IV, 1442. Peter Guthrie Tait, 1831. General Salazar, 1889.

29th   Duke of Wellington, 1769. Jules Henri Poincare, 1854. William Randolph Hearst, 1863. Rafael Sabatini, 1875. Sir Thomas Beecham, 1879. Sir Malcolm

Sargent, 1895. Emperor Hirohito of
Japan, 1901. Tino Rossi, 1907. Renée
Jeanmaire, 1924.

30th   Queen Mary II (wife of William III,
to whom she is always bracketed), 1662.
Franz Lehar, 1870. Queen Juliana of
the Netherlands, 1909.

THE
UPBRINGING
OF APRIL
BABIES
OF
THE
PAST

SOME children should be often
admonished to lay aside a gloomy and
a frowning look, a scowling air, an
uneasy and forbidding aspect. They should
be taught to smooth the ruffles of their
brow, and put on a lively, pleasing, and
cheerful countenance among their friends.
Some there are who have all these graces by
nature, but those who have them not may be

corrected and softened by the care of parents in younger years.

It may here be recollected, by the way, that a gloominess of aspect does not always arise from a malignity of temper, but sometimes from fear of displeasing and incurring reproof, and is therefore often to be removed by speaking kindly to children, and encouraging them with expressions of candour and tenderness. To know how in such cases to divert a child, and make him cheerful and happy in the company of a parent, is none of the least important cares of education.

The Works of the Reverend and Learned
Isaac Watts, D.D., 1810.

The want of affection in the English is strongly manifested towards their children; for after having kept them at home till they arrive at the age of 7 or 9 years at the utmost, they put them out, both males and females, to hard service in the houses of other people, binding them generally for another 7 or 9 years. And these are called apprentices, and during that time they perform all the most menial offices; and few are born who are exempted from this fate, for

every one, however rich he may be, sends away his children into the houses of others, whilst he, in return, receives those of strangers into his own.

And on inquiring their reason for this severity, they answered that they did it in order that their children might learn better manners. But I, for my part, believe that they do it because they like to enjoy all their comforts themselves, and that they are better served by strangers than they would be by their own children.

A Relation of the Island of England,
by an Italian diplomat, about
1500, translated by C. A. Sneyd
for the Camden Society, 1847.

READY-MADE LAYETTE
With Prices

		s.	d.
6	Fine Lawn Shirts	1	9
6	Long Cloth Night Gowns	4	9
6	Hair Cord Monthly Gowns	6	6
2	Muslin Robes, richly trimmed	13	6
1	Muslin Robe, richly trimmed	31	6
4	Tucked Petticoats	3	11
3	Saxony Day Flannels	5	11
3	Welsh Night Flannels	3	11
4	Twill Swathes	1	3
2	Flannel Swathes, with Silk Elastic	2	11
2	Dozen Diapers	10	6
3	Flannel Pilches	2	6

		s.	d.
1	Mackintosh Pilch	2	0
2	Flannel Head Squares	4	6
1	Flannel Wrapper	10	6
6	Quilted Bibs	1	0
2	Pair Knitted Boots	0	9
1	Shetland Veil	2	6
1	Berlin Wool Spencer	2	6
1	Quilted Silk Hood	13	6
1	Braided Cashmere Cloak	31	6

1 Berceaunette, trimmed and fully	s.	d.
fitted	70	0
1 Basket, fully fitted to match	30	0

Bits about Babies,
London, 1870.

On Sunday last . . . between 9 and 10 of
the clock in the morning, a young Girl
about three years of age, strayed away from
her Father; she has on a red Cap, and a
striped Gown, with an Orange-coloured
Petticoat, green Stockins, and a pair of
new Shoes.

The True Domestick Intelligence,
16th April, 1680.

WHEN A CHILD IS ATTACKED

Cut three corners of a table edge from
below, of every edge a chip and a grain of
salt, and a bit of bread, also a little of
buck's beard. All this do noiselessly, and
suspend on the child's neck, with a little
unbleached yarn, during an uneven hour,
and with these words call the child's name,
viz: This I suspend for ransom sake, in the

name of God the Father, the Son, and the
Holy Spirit.

Albertus Magnus, *White and Black
Art for Man and Beast*, 13th Century.
Translated *c.* 1880.

The custom of making fools on the 1st of
April is one of the few old English merriments
still in general vogue. We used to say on the
occasion of having entrapped any one . . .

Fool, fool, April fool,
You learn nought by going to school!
The legitimate period only extends to noon,
and if any one makes an April-fool after that
hour, the boy on whom the attempt is made,
retorts with the distich . . .

> April-fool time's past and gone,
> You're the fool, and I'm none!

Halliwell, *Popular Rhymes and
Nursery Tales*, 1849.

A CUSTOM

In Cheshire, children go round the village and beg for 'an egg, bacon, cheese or an apple, or any good thing to make us merry,' and ending with 'and I pray you, good dame, an Easter egg.' In Cumberland and Westmoreland the same custom prevails, and *pask* or *paste* eggs are reciprocally sent from one friend to another. The mode of preparing the eggs is by plunging them in hot water for a few minutes, and then writing a name or drawing an ornament on the shell with tallow; the egg is then boiled in water containing any coloured dye in solution; this colour will not attach itself to the shell in any part which has been covered with grease, and consequently all the ornaments will appear white. Another method, which requires more skill and labour, is to stain the egg of an uniform colour, and scratch out the ornament or name by means of a penknife.

The Easter eggs, which are stained of an uniform colour, afford amusement to the children in a sort of game, in which the strength of the egg-shell is tested. The boy, holding an egg in his hand, challenges a companion to give blow for blow; one of the eggs is sure to be broken, and its shattered remains are the spoil of the conqueror, whose egg assumes a consequence in proportion to the number of times it has escaped unbroken. To obtain an egg, which, when boiled, shall be as hard as possible, the boys are in the habit of watching the hen when she lays, taking the egg immediately from under her, and boiling it at once; by this means the white of the egg becomes harder than if it were boiled at a future time.

Howitt, *Pictorial Calendar of the Seasons*, 1854.

TWO
ROYAL APRIL
BABIES

MARY, sixth daughter of King Edward the First and Queen Eleanor, was born at Windsor, April the 12th, 1279. Being but ten years of age, she was made a nun at Amesbury in Wiltshire without her own, and at the first against her parents' consent, merely to gratify queen [dowager] Eleanor her grandmother. Let us pity her, who probably did not pity herself, as not knowing a veil from a kerchief; not understanding the requisites to, nor her own fitness for, that profession; having afterwards time too much to bemoan, but none to amend, her condition.

Fuller, *The History of the Worthies of England*, 1840.

Catharine the First of Russia was born on 5th April, 1689. She was called Martha as a child, and at the age of three ... 'the poor Infant was abandoned, as it were, to the miserable Care of the Vicar, who had answered for her at her Baptism. One Day as M. Gluck,

Superintendant of Marienbourg, called at the Vicar of Ringen's in his Way to Dorpt, the Vicar made Complaint to him of the poor Condition he was in, and among other Things, of his being obliged to maintain this Foundling, shewing him young Martha, who began to be a well-made Lass with a happy Physiognomy. The Superintendant Gluck, touch'd with the poor Condition of the Vicar, was willing to relieve him of this Burden; and at his Return to Marienbourg, took the Girl with him, to whom he gave the Care of dressing his Children, and waiting upon them to Church. She was treated in this Family better than a common Servant, and remained in that Condition till the eighteenth Year of her Age, growing every Day handsomer and handsomer.'

Mottley, *The History of the Life and Reign of the Empress Catharine*,

1744.

AN APRIL EMPEROR

LOUIS NAPOLEON
born April 1808.

When but four years old, he, for the first time, beheld a chimney-sweep, all black with soot. The strange sight greatly alarmed him, so that he rushed to his governess, and sought her protection. Madame de Bouhers, acting on the theories of Jean Jacques, which were then so much in vogue, took the opportunity of 'improving the occasion,' by inculcating the moral lesson of self-command. She did not do this violently, or even reprove her charge, but took her pupil on her knee, soothed him with caresses, and by this gentle treatment for ever dissipated the apprehension of sooty boys, for whom she inspired in his mind sentiments of pity. Some months later, when asleep with his brother in the nursery, the nurse retired for a short time. During her absence down popped a young Savoyard from the chimney, wrapped in a sooty envelope. Louis being a light sleeper, awoke, and was again terror-struck at the unexpected apparition. There stood the sweep in his presence, filling the room with a cloud of dust. However, the boy, calling to mind the pitiful tale told him by his governess, soon got composed, left his bed, and running across the room in his night-shirt, climbed on a chair, and having taken his pocket-money from a drawer, gave it, purse and all, to the poor sweep. He then endeavoured to get back to his bed, but failed in the attempt, so that he awoke his brother, who called the nurse to his assistance.

Day, *The True Story of Louis Napoleon's Life*, 1871.

DISTINGUISHED
APRIL
BABIES

HERE is an extract from the school register of the Clergy Daughters' School, Casterton: 'Charlotte Brontë. Entered August 10, 1824. Writes indifferently. Ciphers a little, and works neatly. Knows nothing of grammar, geography, history, or accomplishments. Altogether clever of her age, but knows

nothing systematically. Left school June 1st,
1825 . . . Governess.'

Journal of Education, January, 1900.

THE DUKE OF WELLINGTON
born April 1769.

Unlike boys of his age, he was never seen
to play, but generally came lagging out of
the school-room into the playground; in the
centre of it was a large walnut-tree, against
which he used to lean, observing his

school-fellows, who were playing a variety of games around him. If any boy played unfairly the game he was engaged in, Arthur quickly gave intelligence of it to those who were his playmates; on the delinquent being turned out, it was generally wished that Arthur should supply the place, but nothing could induce him to do so; and when beset by a party of five or six, he would fight with the utmost courage and determination until he freed himself from their grasp; then he would retire to his tree again, and look about him, as quiet, dejected, and observant as he had been before.

Biographical Memoranda of
Arthur Duke of Wellington,
London, 1853.

EDWARD GIBBON
born April 1731.

In January 1746 . . .

'I was sent to Kingston-upon-Thames, to a school of about seventy boys, which was kept by Dr Wooddeson and his assistants. Every time I have since passed over Putney common, I have always noticed the spot where my mother, as we drove along in the coach, admonished me that I was now going into the world, and must learn to think and act for myself. The expression may appear ludicrous,

yet there is not in the course of life a more remarkable change than the removal of a child from the luxury and freedom of a wealthy house to the frugal diet and strict subordination of a school; from the tenderness of parents, and obsequiousness of servants, to the rude familiarity of his equals,

the insolent tyranny of his seniors, and
the rod perhaps of a cruel and capricious
pedagogue. Such hardships may steel the
mind and body against the injuries of fortune;
but my timid reserve was astonished by the
crowd and tumult of the school; the want of
strength and activity disqualified me for the
sports of play-field; nor have I forgotten how
often in the year forty-six I was reviled and
buffeted for the sins of my Tory ancestors. By
the common methods of discipline, at the
expense of many tears and some blood, I
purchased the knowledge of the Latin syntax:
and not long since I was possessed of the
dirty volumes of Phaedrus and Cornelius
Nepos, which I painfully construed and
darkly understood.'

Memoirs of the Life and Writings
of Edward Gibbon, 1827.

ANTHONY TROLLOPE
born April 1815.

My two elder brothers had been sent as
day-boarders to Harrow School from
the bigger house, and may probably have
been received among the aristocratic
crowd, . . . not on equal terms, because a
day-boarder at Harrow in those days was
never so received, . . . but at any rate as other

day-boarders. I do not suppose that they were well treated, but I doubt whether they were subjected to the ignominy which I endured. I was only seven, and I think that boys at seven are now spared among their more considerate seniors. I was never spared; and was not even allowed to run to and fro between our house and the school without a daily purgatory. No doubt my appearance was against me. I remember well, when I was still the junior boy in the school, Dr Butler, the headmaster, stopping me in the street, and asking me, with all the clouds of Jove upon his brow, and all the thunder in his voice, whether it was possible that Harrow School was disgraced by so disreputably dirty a little boy as I! Oh, what I felt at that moment! But I could not look my feelings. I do not doubt that I was dirty; . . . but I think that he was cruel. He must have known me had he seen me as he was wont to see me, for he was in the habit of flogging me constantly. Perhaps he did not recognise me by my face.

Trollope, *An Autobiography*, 1883.

WILLIAM WORDSWORTH
born April 1770.

Speaking of his mother . . .

'An intimate friend of hers, Miss Hamilton
by name, who was used to visit her at
Cockermouth, told me that she once said to
her, that the only one of her five children
about whose future life she was anxious, was
William; and he, she said, would be
remarkable either for good or for evil. The
cause of this was, that I was of a stiff,
moody, and violent temper; so much so that
I remember going once into the attics of my
grandfather's house at Penrith, upon some
indignity having been put upon me, with an
intention of destroying myself with one of
the foils which I knew was kept there. I
took the foil in hand, but my heart failed.
Upon another occasion, while I was at my
grandfather's house at Penrith, along with
my eldest brother, Richard, we were
whipping tops together in the large drawing-
room, on which the carpet was only laid
down upon particular occasions. The walls
were hung round with family pictures, and I

said to my brother, "Dare you strike your whip through that old lady's petticoat?" He replied, "No, I won't." "Then," said I, "here goes;" and I struck my lash through her hooped petticoat, for which no doubt, though I have forgotten it, I was properly punished. But possibly, from some want of judgment in punishments inflicted, I had become perverse and obstinate in defying chastisement, and rather proud of it than otherwise.'

Memoirs of William Wordsworth, 1851.

HANS CHRISTIAN ANDERSEN
born April 1805.

As a child in Odense . . .

'Every circumstance around me tended to excite my imagination . . . The guilds walked in procession through the town with their harlequin before them with mace and bells; on Shrove Tuesday the butchers led the fattest ox through the streets adorned with garlands, whilst a boy in a white shirt and with great wings on his shoulders rode upon it; the sailors paraded through the city with music

and all their flags flying, and then two of the boldest among them stood and wrestled upon a plank placed between two boats, and the one who was not thrown into the water was the victor.

That, however, which more particularly stamped itself upon my memory, and became refreshed by after often-repeated relations, was, the abode of the Spaniards in Funen in 1808. It is true that at that time I was but three years old; still I nevertheless perfectly remember the foreign men who made disturbances in the streets, and the cannon which were fired. I saw the people lying on straw in a half-tumbledown church, which was near the asylum. One day, a Spanish soldier took me in his arms and pressed a silver image, which he wore upon his breast, to my lips. I remember that my mother was angry at it, because, she said, there was something papistical about it; but the image, and the strange man, who danced me about, kissed me and wept, pleased me; certainly he had children at home in Spain.'

Andersen, *The True Story of my Life*, translated by Howitt, 1847.

GAMES
for the
APRIL
BABY

TAKE the two feet of the infant,
and make them go quickly up and
down and over each other, saying
the following appropriate verses:
  'Feetikin, feetikin,
When will ye gang?'
  'When the nichts turn short
And the days turn lang,
    I'll toddle and gang, toddle
      and gang,' etc.
                    Popular Rhymes of Scotland,
                    collected by Chambers, 1842.

THE SEE-SAW

Young children need to be taught how to play even at that properly. First, they must be taught to balance each other. Then to set it going with their feet. It is well if they can be taught to sing some verses as they play. For example:

'See, saw, Margery Daw;
The oldest old woman that ever I saw;
Up we go, up we go, into the sky;
Down we come, down we come, down we come, down from on high!'

Kingston, *Infant Amusements*, 1867.

AN
APRIL
CHILD
IN
FICTION

68

ME, she had dispensed from joining the group; saying, 'She regretted to be under the necessity of keeping me at a distance; but that until she heard from Bessie, and could discover by her own observation that I was endeavouring in good earnest to acquire a more sociable and child-like disposition, a more attractive and sprightly manner, . . . something lighter, franker, more natural as it were . . . she really must exclude me from privileges intended only for contented, happy, little children.'

'What does Bessie say I have done?' I asked.

'Jane, I don't like cavillers or questioners: besides, there is something truly forbidding in a child taking up her elders in that manner. Be seated somewhere; and until you can speak pleasantly, remain silent.'

A small breakfast-room adjoined the drawing-room: I slipped in there. It contained a bookcase: I soon possessed myself of a volume, taking care that it should be one

stored with pictures. I mounted into the window-seat: gathering up my feet, I sat cross-legged, like a Turk; and, having drawn the red moreen curtain nearly close, I was shrined in double retirement.

Charlotte Brontë, *Jane Eyre*, 1847.

LETTERS
from
APRIL
CHILDREN

born April 1593.

TO his deere and lovinge Mother Mrs Margaret Radcliffe, at Thornhill in Yorkshire.

GOOD MOTHER,

Having little time, and the weather verie cold, I am constrained to write both briefly and ilfavouredly. First, therefore, as my duty byndes me, I humblie crave your dayly prayers unto Almighty God for me, and I humblie and hartilie thank you for all kindnesse towards me. Comminge to Longley on Sunday the weather was not verie cold, for we was warm by reason of our much goinge on foote; when we came thither we was very welcome, for both Sir R. Bellamounte and Mr Pilkington and Mr Ramsdens were verie kindlie. On Monday the morning was verie calme: going by the way we called at my Uncle's, but they were gone; we lighted at Marsden, and sate there; cominge to Peele and Staninge the wynde was so boysterous that we could hardly stand, and being both cold and some of us half sick we went to Saddleworth on Monday at night, and there we stayed all night: the next morning was very windy

till noon: at noon we set forth, and so came we (God be thanked!) at Oldham in the afternoon. We are all in good health (praysed be God!) here at Oldham. I pray you send the licorice within this fortnight, pounds 8. My Master would gladlie come to Wakefield if he could get the Schoole: I have heard some commendations of him that hath it (a good while since), but now I heare he is a very proud swaggering fellowe. Thus with my hartiest re'mendations to all our good friends I take my leave.

Oldham, this Wednesday January 13th, 1607.

Your most loving and most obedient sonne,

GEORGE RADCLIFFE.

Whitaker, *The Life and Original Correspondence of Sir George Radcliffe*, 1810.

CHARLOTTE BRONTË
born April 1816.

To the Rev. P. Brontë, Parsonage House, Crosstone, September 23rd, 1829.

MY DEAR PAPA —

At Aunt's request I write these lines to inform you that 'if all be well' we shall be at home on Friday by dinner-time, when we hope to find you in good health. On account of the bad weather we have not been out much, but notwithstanding we have spent our time very pleasantly, between reading, working, and learning our lessons, which Uncle Fennell has been so kind as to teach us every day. Branwell has taken two sketches from nature, and Emily, Anne, and myself have likewise each of us drawn a piece from some views of the lakes which Mr. Fennell brought with him from Westmoreland. The whole of these he intends keeping. Mr. Fennell is sorry he cannot accompany us to Haworth on Friday, for want of room, but hopes to have the pleasure of seeing you soon.

All unite in sending their kind love with your affectionate daughter,

CHARLOTTE BRONTË.

Shorter, *Charlotte Brontë and her Circle*, 1896

RHYMES
for the
APRIL
BABY

APRIL brings the primrose
      sweet,
Scatters daisies at our feet.
            Sara Coleridge (1802–1852).

Our birth is but a sleep and a forgetting:
The Soul that rises with us, our life's Star,
Hath had elsewhere its setting,
    And cometh from afar:
Not in entire forgetfulness,
And not in utter nakedness,
But trailing clouds of glory do we come
    From God, who is our home:
Heaven lies about us in our infancy!

Shades of the prison-house begin to close
  Upon the growing Boy,
But he beholds the light, and whence it
  flows,
  He sees it in his joy;
The Youth, who daily farther from the east
  Must travel, still is Nature's Priest,
    And by the vision splendid
    Is on his way attended;
At length the Man perceives it die away,
  And fade into the light of common day.
             Wordsworth (1770–1850).

Flash forth, thou Sun,
  The rain is over and gone, its work is
  done.

Winter is past,
  Sweet Spring is come at last, is come at
  last.

Bud, Fig and Vine,
  Bud, Olive, fat with fruit and oil and wine.

Break forth this morn
  In roses, thou but yesterday a Thorn.

Uplift thy head,
  O pure white Lily through the Winter
  dead.

Beside your dams
  Leap and rejoice, you merry-making
  Lambs.

All Herds and Flocks
  Rejoice, all Beasts of thickets and of rocks.

Sing, Creatures, sing,
  Angels and Men and Birds and everything.

All notes of Doves
  Fill all our world: this is the time of loves.
          Christina Rossetti (1830–1894).

A PRAYER

Teach me
Thy way,
O Lord.

Psalm 27, verse 11.

GOODNIGHT
to the
APRIL
BABY

82

APRIL is a lovely month in which to be born, for it is the great birth month. The fields are full of newly born lambs. Each hedge hides a nest with a mother bird in careful attendance. Calves, never to look so delightful again, are being licked clean by their mothers until their baby hair stands out in a soft fuzz. On the beaches anxious seagull mothers are laying their eggs made to match as nearly as possible the pebbles around them. The instinct of mother birds and beasts is merely to teach their babies how to survive, for as far as is known cows and sheep never dream that their little sons and daughters may grow up to be national cattle show winners,

and birds, it is understood, never consider
their children as prospective warbling champions.
But you? Are you dreaming of the man or
woman you hope your baby will grow up to
be? Or are you saying, 'No, darling, I've no
plans for you. I want you just the way you are'?

Noel Streatfeild